Sports
Swimming

by Nick Rebman

FOCUS READERS

www.focusreaders.com

Focus Readers is distributed by North Star Editions:
sales@northstareditions.com | 888-417-0195

Produced for Focus Readers by Red Line Editorial.

Photographs ©: I love photo/Shutterstock Images, cover, 1; Golden Pixels LLC/Shutterstock Images, 4; phdpsx/iStockphoto, 7; wavebreakmedia/Shutterstock Images, 9, 15, 16 (top left), 16 (bottom right); Red Tiger/Shutterstock Images, 11; rayna/iStockphoto, 13; Snapper 68/Shutterstock Images, 16 (top right); YanLev/Shutterstock Images, 16 (bottom left)

ISBN
978-1-63517-923-1 (hardcover)
978-1-64185-025-4 (paperback)
978-1-64185-227-2 (ebook pdf)
978-1-64185-126-8 (hosted ebook)

Library of Congress Control Number: 2018931989

Printed in the United States of America
Mankato, MN
May, 2018

About the Author

Nick Rebman enjoys reading, drawing, and traveling to places where he doesn't speak the language. He lives in Minnesota.

Table of Contents

Swimming

Swimming is fun.

People swim in a **pool**.

Swimmers wear **suits**.

Some swimmers

wear **goggles**.

Goggles keep eyes dry.

Safety

Swimmers must stay safe.

They do not swim alone.

An **adult** must be near.

adult

How to Swim

This swimmer is on his back.

He moves his arms.

He moves his legs.

These swimmers race.

They try to swim fast.

The fastest one wins.

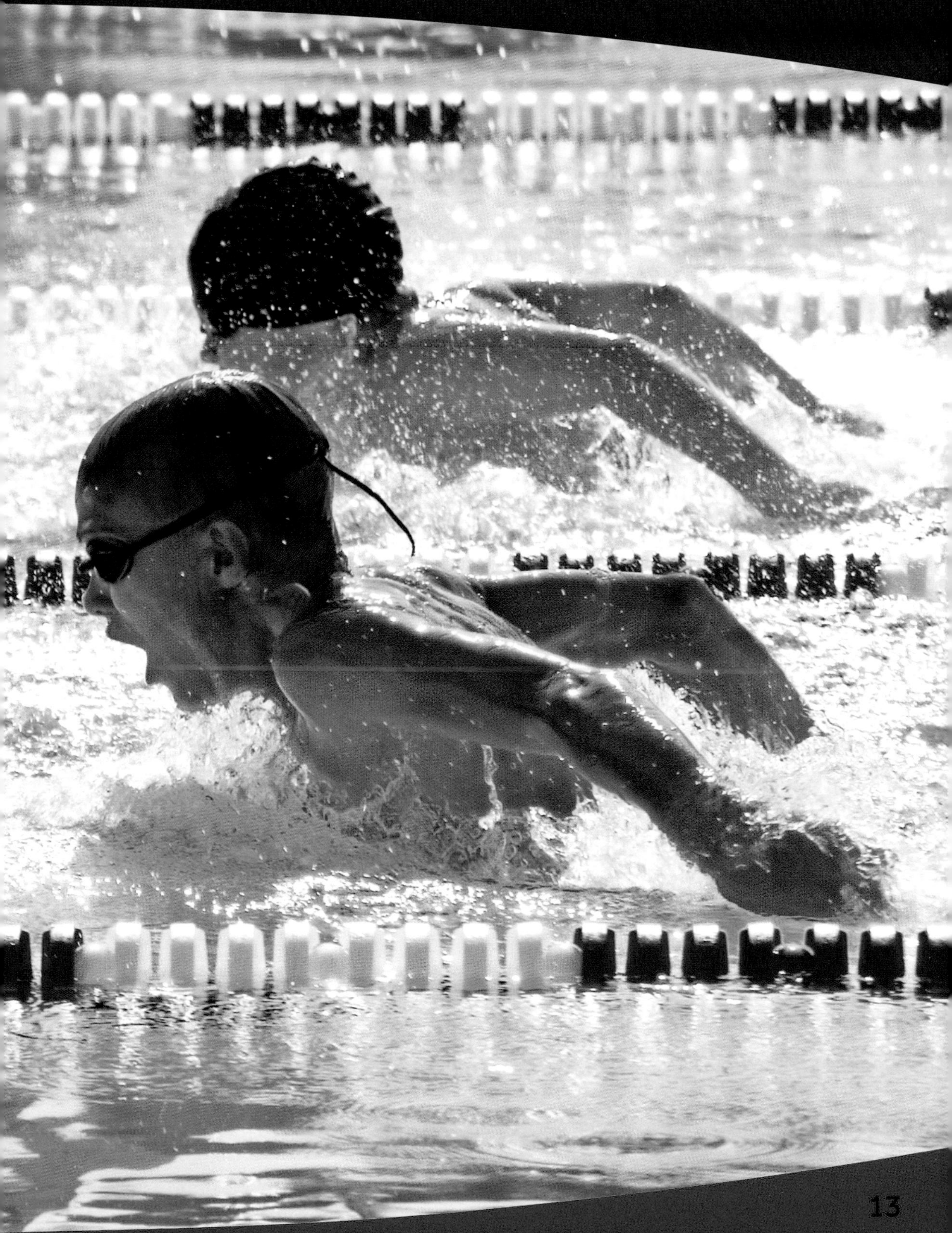

There are many ways

to swim.

They are all fun to learn.

Glossary

adult

pool

goggles

suits

Index